THE WORLD HERITAGE

PREHISTORIC
STONE MONUMENTS

CHILDRENS PRESS®
CHICAGO

Table of Contents

Introduction 4
The Beginnings of Agriculture 6
Timeline 8
The Builders of the Dolmens 10
The Age of Metals 14
Special Terms 14
Stonehenge and Avebury 22
Stonehenge and King Arthur 24
The Temples of Ggantija 26
The Hypogeum of Hal Saflieni 28
Glossary 32
Index 33

Library of Congress Cataloging-in-Publication

Martin, Ana.
   [Sitos megalitcos. English]
   Prehistoric stone monuments / by Ana Martin.
      p. cm. — (The World heritage)
    Includes index.
    Summary: Explores the origins and significance of the great stone monuments
dating from the Neolithic Age which are found throughout Western Europe.
    ISBN 0-516-08386-4
    1. Megalithic monuments—Europe—Juvenile literature. 2. Europe—Antiquities—
Juvenile literature. [1. Megalithic monuments—Europe. 2. Europe—Antiquities.]
I. Title. II. Series.
GN790.M3813 1993
936—dc20

             93-756
             CIP
             AC

Sitos megaliticos: © INCAFO S.A./Ediciones S.M./UNESCO 1991
Prehistoric Stone Monuments: © Childrens Press, Inc./UNESCO 1993

ISBN (UNESCO) 92-3-102686-0
ISBN (Childrens Press) 0-516-08386-4

Prehistoric Stone Monuments

From the British Isles to Malta, Western Europe is dotted with strange stone monuments that are sometimes referred to as megaliths. The term megalithic comes from the Greek words mega, *meaning great, and* litos, *meaning stone. Megalithic monuments are made of enormous blocks of stone. In some cases, a single stone may weigh many tons.*

The origin of these monuments has long been a mystery. It seemed that only superhuman force could move such massive stones. For this reason, numerous legends have arisen, telling of a race of giants who inhabited the world before the arrival of human beings.

Nevertheless, the monuments were erected by people who lived in the Neolithic Age, many thousands of years ago. More ancient than the Egyptian pyramids or the first cities of ancient Sumeria, these enormous stone monuments represent humanity's earliest architectural achievements. Their creators had made a great leap in human history. They gave up being nomadic hunters to become settled farmers.

From the Mediterranean to the Atlantic
Thousands of miles separate Malta from the British Isles. The space between them is known today as Western Europe. Yet six thousand years ago, this distance was united by a single cultural concept. Its most notable feature was the use of enormous blocks of stone for constructing religious and funerary monuments. Among the best-known are the stone circles at Stonehenge in England *(top)*, and the Maltese temples of Ggantija *(bottom)*.

The Beginnings of Agriculture

About 12,000 years ago, somewhere in the Middle East, people developed a new way of life: agriculture and herding. They learned to cultivate plants they could eat and to domesticate some of the wild animals they hunted. This change marked the beginning of a new epoch, called the Neolithic Age. Many other important changes in human history took place in those times. Until then, people had lived as nomads, following great herds of herbivores on their migrations and gathering edible plants that they found along the way. They lived in caves or shelters made of branches and animal skins. Their only possessions were a few stone tools, weapons, and religious figurines.

With the development of agriculture, this way of life changed radically. To cultivate a field, the farmer had to settle nearby, at least until harvest time. The nomads became sedentary. They abandoned their caves and built more comfortable huts of wood. The first villages emerged. People learned to make clay vessels in which to store the food they raised. From flax and cotton fibers, they wove clothing that was much more comfortable than the animal skins they had worn before. Their possessions increased as they needed more tools for these activities: axes to cut down forests, hoes and spades for working in the fields. For a long time, these tools were made of stone.

A Technical Problem

Historians have not yet solved the mystery of how these huge stones were set in place. At Carnac in Bretagne *(left)*, the stones are arranged in lines. At Stonehenge in England *(right)*, they are arranged in circles. It is thought that they were hauled from quarries and transported on log rollers. Then they may have been lifted with cords and pulleys until the base settled into a hole, which was then packed in with stones and earth. Of course, this would take a great number of people and a great amount of time.

People no longer had to search for food every day. Free time was available for art, festivals, or religious rituals.

At first, agriculture and domestic animals coexisted with hunting and gathering. But as the variety and number of cultivated plants and domesticated animals grew, hunting and gathering were gradually abandoned.

As agricultural methods were perfected, people became capable of producing more food than they needed to live. This had two important results. First, it was no longer necessary for everyone in the community to work in the fields. Some people became artisans, specialists in making clay vessels, baskets, or stone tools. They traded these goods with the peasants in exchange for food. Later, there were priests who tended to religious rituals, warriors who defended the villages, and traders who exchanged products with other regions.

Second, because nutrition improved, people lived longer and the population increased. Now some individuals set out in search of new lands to farm. On their travels they met nomadic peoples to whom they taught their farming techniques. Thus agriculture spread across Europe, Asia, and Africa. By about 5000 B.C., it was being practiced all around the Mediterranean; before 4000 B.C. it had reached the Atlantic coast; and 500 years later, it arrived in the British Isles.

During this period, the first cities flourished in Mesopotamia, an ancient region in present-day Iraq. Inhabitants of these cities knew how to use metals, developed a form of writing, and watered their fields using a complex system of canals. The Neolithic Period had passed into the Bronze Age, which still took many years to reach Europe's Atlantic coast.

Timeline

10,000 B.C.	Beginning of agriculture in the Middle East.
6000 B.C.	Discovery of the metallurgy of copper and gold.
5000 B.C.	Agriculture spreads throughout Europe.
4800 B.C.	Construction of the Dolmen of Kerkado in Bretagne, France, the oldest in Europe.
3000 B.C.	Discovery of bronze in Mesopotamia.
2500 B.C.	Megalithic monuments of Malta are built. Metallurgy of copper extends throughout Europe. Construction of Stonehenge begins.
1500 B.C.	Bronze replaces copper all over Europe. The last phase of Stonehenge begins.
1000 B.C.	The use of iron begins to spread across Europe.

The Culture of Stone
How did Neolithic people acquire the technological skill revealed in their great monuments? They may have begun constructing buildings with wood or mud. Later they may have translated or transformed these forms to stone. The pictures here show the entrance to South Temple of Ggantija *(right)* and a view of Stonehenge *(below)*, two advanced works of megalithic architecture.

The Builders of the Dolmens

The first European farmers did not live in villages. Instead, they built their scattered wooden huts beside their fields. They raised chiefly grains: wheat, barley, rye, and oats. In addition, they grew peas, lentils, and other legumes. They had sheep, goats, and pigs, which grazed and foraged in the surrounding forests. The people were organized into tribes, each composed of various clans whose members were thought to be descendants of a common ancestor. They honored their dead chiefs, burying them in magnificent stone tombs that were then covered with earth, forming a mound.

These tombs are the first known megalithic monuments. Depending on the region and structure, they have various names. The simplest are the dolmens, consisting of a few upright stones covered with a large flat slab. So-called passage-graves have an access corridor that leads to the funerary chamber, as in the famous Caves of Antequera in Spain. The West Kennett Tomb in England consists of five chambers used for multiple burials over several periods.

For a long time it was believed that such constructions originated in the Middle East, along with agriculture and herding. But today we know that the oldest dolmens were built in the Bretagne region of France, one of the westernmost points in Europe, between 4600 and 4000 B.C. In fact, archaeologists believe that the construction of such huge stone monuments began in Europe itself, probably in several places at once.

The importance given to these tombs reveals much about the mentality of Neolithic people. They must have had a solid social organization. It requires great coordination among many people to move such enormous stones solely by human effort. It is also apparent that they had some type of religious belief. The fact that people were buried with their weapons and most valuable tools indicates that they believed in another life where these instruments would be needed. Some megalithic tombs have inscriptions and paintings that could represent sacred objects: sun symbols, torches, or images of gods and goddesses.

These beliefs, and the rituals connected with them, grew more complicated with the passage of time. In addition to tombs, megalithic temples have been found on the island of Malta in the Mediterranean Sea. These temples seem to have been used in complex ceremonies. They belong to a later period, around 2500 B.C., about 2,000 years after the first dolmens were erected on the European continent. They had spread from the mainland to Malta.

Mysterious Sun Cults
The people who built Stonehenge worshiped the sun, so vital to a farming community. They thoroughly understood the course of the sun throughout the seasons of the year. Built in accord with this knowledge, the monument is a gigantic calendar. It was probably also the scene of rituals during the summer solstice. At this time, the first ray of the sun passes over the heelstone (shown in the top photo) across one of the trilithons.

New Ways of Life

The shift from the Paleolithic to the Neolithic Age produced great changes in everyday European life. The cultivation and harvesting of grain became a principal activity, though hunting and the gathering of wild fruits and honey persisted. This is clear in the cave paintings that abound in certain regions of Spain. This portrayal of a deer hunt appears on a cave wall in Valltorta, Castile.

Everyday household objects also changed markedly. Paleolithic people made simple, useful things: stones sharpened with blows and bows of carved bone. In the Neolithic Age, ceramic pottery appeared, in an array of shapes and decorative styles. The bell-shaped pot was one of its most extreme variations. The arrival of metals allowed the addition of luxury items, such as crescent-shaped ornamental collars and finely worked gold jewelry.

A new culture began to spread throughout the eastern Mediterranean region, perhaps originating in the island of Crete. One of the main features of this culture was its use of bronze; another was the importance it placed on religion and religious rituals. From this time forward, megalithic monuments would not be used for burial alone, but would shelter the ceremonies of the living.

The Age of Metals

Archaeologists believe that sometime around 6000 B.C., in the region of present-day Turkey, Iran, and Iraq, people made a discovery even more revolutionary than agriculture. This discovery was the use of metal. At first it developed slowly. The first known metals, copper and gold, were used only for ornamentation. But finally, after a thousand years and many experiments, people learned to make copper tools and weapons. Although this was a great advance, copper was not durable enough to replace stone completely. Both materials coexisted for some time. Gold was still used for ornaments, and owning it became a symbol of prestige.

Special Terms

ablution: purification by means of water, a rite in some religions.

alloy: metal resulting from smelting together two or more other metals.

apse: visible external part of the altar of a church, usually circular in form. Here the term refers to chambers similar in form and location, but belonging to megalithic temples.

clan: group of families descended from a common ancestor.

hypogeum: from the Greek words *hypo* (under) and *geo* (earth). An underground tomb, similar to those found in ancient Egypt.

lintel: upper part of a doorway, formed by a horizontal piece supported on two vertical pieces.

megalithic: from the Greek words *mega* (great) and *litos* (stone). The name given to prehistoric monuments made of huge stones.

monolith: a huge stone that stands as a monument by itself.

nomad: a person without fixed residence, moving from one place to another.

ossuary: place where bones are buried or deposited.

trilithon: megalithic monument formed of three stones.

tumulus: artificial mound of earth that covers a tomb.

A World Grown Complicated
With the coming of the Bronze Age, society and religion grew more complex. Gods appeared that represented the forces of nature. They had to be appeased with ceremonies performed in sacred places. For this reason, temples were built. The oldest ones have been found in Malta. These include the Hypogeum of Hal Saflieni, decorated with paintings such as the one in the top photo, and the temples of Ggantija *(bottom)*.

Deposits of copper and gold were found in many parts of Europe. They were common enough that, over thousands of years, many groups of people figured out how to use them. By about 2500 B.C., copper was being used throughout Europe. It was also being traded, along routes opened by the first Neolithic farmers.

The real leap forward, however, occurred in Mesopotamia in about 3000 B.C. At that time, people discovered the alloy (mixture) of copper and tin called bronze. Bronze was much harder than either of its two components, and it was easy to mold into tools. The blades of bronze knives, axes, spades, and swords were more easily made than those of stone tools, and bronze was harder than copper. Bronze implements were made to thresh wheat, to cut down trees, and to skin animals. (Experiments have shown, however, that stone tools can be sharper tools than metal ones.)

The use of bronze spread rapidly across Europe. Tin, which was necessary in manufacturing bronze, was not abundant in the Middle East. The increasing demand made it necessary to seek out new sources of tin. The best deposits were in the west — in England, Bretagne, and Galicia. The peoples who lived in these lands learned to use and to trade the mineral they mined. With these changes, society evolved quickly. By about 1500 B.C., bronze had replaced copper throughout Europe.

The people of the Bronze Age lived very differently than their Neolithic ancestors. New trades appeared in relation to the use of metal. There were miners, smelters, and goldsmiths. Compared to stone, metal was rather scarce. To possess it was soon a sign of prestige. This emphasized the differences between some individuals and others. Thus social classes emerged. People now had property to defend. This led them to abandon their scattered settlements and crowd together in fortified towns with solid walls. Bronze weapons were perfected rapidly, and organized armies were created.

In the east, the first great civilizations emerged during this era: the Sumerians in Mesopotamia, the empire of the pharaohs in Egypt, the Minoan culture in Crete. In addition to magnificent works of art, they have all left us abundant written records of their way of life and thought. In Western Europe, on the other hand, culture did not reach such a high level of refinement. We only know how society developed by studying archaeological finds.

The development of irrigation systems, the selective breeding of plants and cattle, and above all, new, more effective bronze tools brought about an increase in food production.

Minorca, a World Apart

The Balearic Islands lie in the western Mediterranean Sea, near the east coast of Spain. During the second millennium B.C., the people there developed a unique culture, different than the culture found in the rest of Europe. The people of the islands were farmers and herders. They had also mastered the techniques of making bronze and constructing megalithic monuments. They may have originated from Sardinia, an island off southern Italy, and they settled mainly on the Balearic island of Minorca. There their culture evolved in isolation over a period of two thousand years, until the Roman conquest. Their towns are still preserved, as are some unique megalithic monuments.

The various types of stone monuments here are called taulas, navetas, and talaiotes. The talaiotes are the most abundant. Round or square in form, they probably served as fortified dwellings. The navetas were used as tombs. Their name comes from the word nave (boat), because they resemble inverted boats. The taulas were composed of two stone slabs, one placed on the other to form a T shape, and surrounded by a wall. It is thought that they served some ritual function, perhaps as the central altar of a temple. This photo shows the taula of Talati.

Just as in Neolithic times, this meant that people had more leisure time. Society could support more individuals whose work was not directly involved with food production. Artists and craftsmen flourished. In addition to potters, stone carvers, and masons, there were bronzesmiths, goldsmiths, musicians, and weavers. The number of soldiers and traders increased, and there were more priests than ever before.

Religion was a key element in Bronze Age society. The community was united by its belief in the same gods or in the practice of the same rituals. At the center of religious life were the priests, who became the most powerful social class.

Under the priests' direction, new megalithic monuments were constructed in this era. They were grander and more finely constructed than those of the Neolithic Age. The new monuments were products of well-organized communities using advanced technical knowledge. Burial tombs were no longer used only for men, but for women and children as well. This shift indicates that society was no longer governed by isolated warrior chiefs. There was now a hereditary privileged class.

The most noteworthy Bronze Age constructions are various formations of huge, upright stones. Such monuments were especially abundant in Bretagne and in southern England. One stunning example is the great assemblage of stones at Carnac, in northwestern France. This grouping consists of some 3,000 monoliths in various parallel rows. Another example is the circle of stones at Stonehenge in England, formed of meticulously carved pieces. Burials have been found at both these sites.

Magic and Religion
Megalithic monuments were built to be part of ancient funerary, religious, and even magical rituals. In the Hypogeum of Hal Saflieni *(left)*, the ceremonies of an unknown cult were performed. The photo on the right shows part of the Line of Carnac, which served as the burial site for a caste of ancient Breton warrior chiefs.

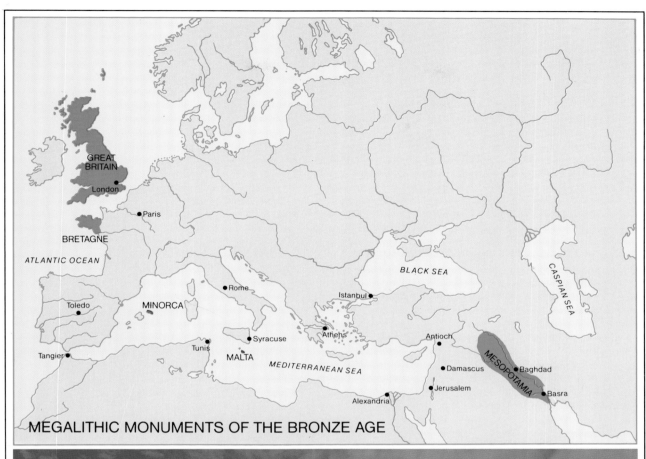

MEGALITHIC MONUMENTS OF THE BRONZE AGE

Megalithic Monuments of Minorca

Some of the impressive stone monuments of the island of Minorca are: the Taliote of Talati *(top left)*; the town of the Tower d'En Gaumes *(top right)*; the Naveta d'Es Tudons *(lower left)*; the Taula of Trepuco *(lower right)*.

The purpose of these monuments is not known. We do know that their builders took into account the movements of the sun and moon in the course of the year. This does not mean, however, that they served as astronomical observatories, as some have claimed. It is more likely that they were the scene of sacred religious rituals practiced by a sun cult.

After the year 1000 B.C., people arrived in Europe who knew the use of iron, a metal much stronger than any used before. Little by little, the Bronze Age drew to a close. Along with iron came new ways of life, new beliefs, and new funeral rituals that no longer included building great stone monuments. The old stone structures were gradually abandoned.

Some centuries later, the Celts spread across Europe. The Celts were a warlike people who also used iron and worshiped the sun and the moon. In Ireland, England, Bretagne, or Galicia they mingled with the descendants of the people who had built dolmens. At times they used these ancient structures in the practice of their own rituals. Thus, many remained standing until the Roman conquest. This marks the end of the Iron Age, and also of European prehistory.

Stonehenge and Avebury

On Salisbury Plain in southern England stands Stonehenge, the most famous of all megalithic sites. These monuments also show the most highly perfected workmanship.

There appear to be three phases of construction, known as I, II, and III. These phases cover a period of about 1,000 years, from 2500 to 1500 B.C.

During the first phase, in the middle of the 3000s B.C., a platform 52 feet (16 meters) in diameter was built, surrounded by an outer circular ditch and bank. Just within the bank was a circle of 56 holes, named "Aubrey's holes" after their discoverer. Some of these were used for burials. In the center of the platform were arranged the four Stones of the Seasons, placed according to the position of the sun at dawn on the summer solstice.

Europe was still in the Neolithic Age when the second phase of Stonehenge began in 1750 B.C. The entrance was widened to an avenue leading to the end stone, or heelstone, just outside the main group. Bluish stones were brought from the Prescelly Mountains in Wales, some 125 miles (200 kilometers) away. They were arranged in two concentric circles on the platform. How these stones were transported is one of the great mysteries of Stonehenge, even today.

The People of Wessex
Like Avebury, Stonehenge III belongs to the "Wessex Cult," which flourished in southwest England during the second millennium B.C. The people of Wessex were good navigators, who traded with the Greeks. It is possible that the builders of Stonehenge learned from the Greeks the methods used to build the colossal tombs in the Greek city of Mycenae.

MEGALITHIC MONUMENTS OF THE UNITED KINGDOM

Orkney Islands

NORTH SEA

Aberdeen

Clyde

Edinburgh

Newcastle

UNITED KINGDOM

Irish Sea

Manchester

Dublin

Liverpool

Birmingham

Thames

Bristol

London

AVEBURY

STONEHENGE

Southampton

English Channel

This second phase was never fully completed. Suddenly it was replaced by a new, more grandiose project, and the blue stones were taken away. The third phase began almost immediately, perhaps before 1720 B.C. For this phase, new stone was brought from a quarry in Marlborough Down, 27 miles (44 kilometers) from Stonehenge. Once carved, they were arranged to form a wide circle covered with a continuous lintel. The 30 vertical uprights and the horizontal blocks were ingeniously fitted together.

In the center of the circle stood five great trilithons. Each of these structures was formed of three stones in the form of an inverted *U*. The trilithons were arranged in a semicircle, so that only one opening led to the interior. At dawn on the morning of the summer solstice, the first ray of sun precisely penetrates this point, after passing over the heelstone, to reach the very center of the semicircle formed by the trilithons.

Later, in the Bronze Age, the monument underwent some minor changes. Some of the blue stones from Prescelly were recovered and put in the space outlined by the five trilithons. The structure then consisted of three concentric circles of upright stones.

Tomb of Legendary Kings
This reconstruction of Stonehenge shows how it looked in its completed form. This is how it was when the Celts first knew it, and later the Romans. Both peoples must have been impressed by its grandiose appearance. It is not surprising that they thought it the work of giants or the tomb of the most illustrious kings of ancient Britain.

The picture above depicts the legend of King Arthur and Merlin the Magician.

Stonehenge and King Arthur

When the Romans conquered England in the first century A.D., they found it occupied by a Celtic people called the Britons. Their priests, the Druids, performed ceremonies of the sun cult at Stonehenge. But the Druids themselves did not know the origins of the monument, which was already one thousand years old when they reached the island. Over time, the mysterious circle of stones entered Celtic legend. It was especially important in the most famous legend of them all: the story of King Arthur.

The legend of King Arthur draws on historical fact, particularly the glories of a fifth-century Briton leader who defended his country against the Saxon invaders. But fact is blended with elements from a variety of older Celtic tales.

One of these stories describes how Uther Pendragon, Arthur's father, traveled to Ireland in search of the Giants' Circle, a group of magic stones with healing powers. He defeated the Irish in a battle and, with the help of Merlin the Magician, brought the stones by boat to England. Raised once more on Mount Ambrio, on Salisbury Plain, they served as funerary monuments for the British knights killed in the struggle with the Saxons. Later, Uther Pendragon himself would be buried there.

Naturally, the Giants' Circle is none other than Stonehenge. The legend of its journey seems to have very ancient roots. Perhaps it gives us a clue to the way the blue stones were transported from Prescelly in Wales.

After the site was abandoned (no one knows precisely when this occurred), many of the stones toppled. But enough remain standing to give us an idea how impressive the whole structure must have been from the avenue that leads to the heelstone.

Many other megalithic monuments of the same period can be found throughout southern England. One of the most important is the Avebury Circle. It is located not far from Stonehenge and is composed of the same stone from Marlborough Down. The two structures are similar, but Avebury is larger. It is less well preserved, however, and it has been impossible to reconstruct its original structure. Unlike Stonehenge, it had a small wooden structure at its center, perhaps a temple.

The Temples of Ggantija

On the little island of Gozo, one of the three islands that make up Malta, stands the monument of Ggantija. It consists of two temples surrounded by a wall.

Both temples belong to the Bronze Age, which began very early in Malta, sometime between 3000 and 2000 B.C. The oldest and best preserved is the South Temple, consisting of a patio from which open three apses. This structure is typical of Maltese temples. A large stone slab at the entrance could have been an altar, and the hollowed-out stone beside it may have been used by priests for ritual ablutions (washings). Ashes have been found in the apses, perhaps the remains of a "sacred fire." Another altar may have been used for sacrifices. It has holes through which blood might have poured. The total picture suggests a religion based on the forces of nature. This is similar to belief systems of other Mediterranean communities at that time.

The Work of Giants
Ggantija means "Tower of the Giants." According to legend, these fabulous beings built the temples (*right*) on the tiny island of Gozo. Some of its stones weighed up to 50 tons. Inside, altars have been found that seem to have been used in fertility rites and animal sacrifices.

MEGALITHIC MONUMENTS OF MALTA

MEDITERRANEAN SEA

GGANTIJA

Ggantija • • Nadur

Island of Gozo ◁ Island of Comino

Mellieha •
St. Paul's Bay • HAL SAFLIENI
• Valletta
Rabat •

Island of Malta • Birzebbuga

MEDITERRANEAN SEA

The more recent North Temple has a similar structure. It consists of two patios. The first opens from two wide apses, and the second from a smaller apse where the main altar was located. Though it is less well preserved than South Temple, many of the walls are still standing. They are formed from blocks of granite 16 feet (5 meters) high and weighing fifty tons apiece.

We know little of the people who built these temples. We can only study other ancient Maltese remains and compare these finds with those from other places. At the end of the Bronze Age, around 2000 B.C., people left the island of Gozo for unknown reasons. Many centuries passed before Malta was inhabited again.

The Hypogeum of Hal Saflieni

This monument is unusual in that it is entirely underground. It is found on the island of Malta, not far from Valletta, the capital. It is called a hypogeum, meaning an underground burial chamber. But unlike the Egyptian tombs, it is a temple rather than a burial site.

Like the temples of Ggantija, it belongs to the Bronze Age. Its structure is more complex, though, showing that it dates from a later period. Nevertheless, no metal tools were used in building it. With only primitive equipment such as stone tools and carved deer antlers, three underground levels were excavated to form this complex.

The Maltese Labyrinth
On the island of Crete there existed a famous labyrinth, or maze of corridors. At the center, as legend tells, there lived the terrible Minotaur—half man and half raging bull. The people of Malta constructed a labyrinth of their own in the Hypogeum of Hal Saflieni. Its structure is a true chaos of underground rooms and passages. Perhaps it was meant to frustrate intruders who tried to reach the sanctuary of the god.

The upper level consists of a series of natural grottoes, where religious ceremonies were performed. Below extends a second level, entirely built by humans. It consists of a series of rooms and passages, seemingly arranged like a maze. One of these, the so-called "Oracle Room," can distort the human voice, causing a strange echo effect. This chamber may have been used in some ritual.

The third level has a series of smaller rooms. Because it is somewhat hidden, some think it may have been the true temple of Hal Saflieni.

Outside, right above the hypogeum, stand the ruins of a building that contained the entrance to the underground temple. We do not know if it was constructed before or after the hypogeum itself.

After serving as the scene of religious ceremonies for a long time, the twenty or so chambers of the hypogeum were converted to an ossuary, or bone depository. Excavations there have revealed the remains of some 7,000 people.

Europe's Memory
Huge prehistoric stone monuments, or megaliths, are a unique testimony to the origins of European architecture. Thus UNESCO has chosen several notable monument sites as World Heritage sites. These include the Maltese sanctuaries of Ggantija *(opposite page, top left)* and Hal Saflieni *(left; and opposite page, bottom left),* and the circles at Stonehenge *(opposite page, right)* and Avebury in Great Britain.

Underground Architecture
Although carved entirely in rock, the interior decoration of Hal Saflieni *(left)* reveals some unique elements of megalithic architecture. These include this false trilithon that seems to support the access door to one of the rooms.

These Sites Are Part of the World Heritage

Monuments of Stonehenge and Avebury: These are the most important megalithic monuments in England. They were built during the transition to the Bronze Age (2500-1500 B.C.). They consist of great stone circles, carefully carved and set upright, then placed in accord with the positions of the sun and the moon.

Temples of Ggantija: Located on the island of Gozo in the republic of Malta, they are two temples from the Bronze Age (3000-2000 B.C.), enclosed by a common wall. Both are typical Maltese temples in structure, with three round apses opening off central patios.

Hypogeum of Hal Saflieni: This is the only underground religious building on the island of Malta. It consists of three levels carved into the rock, the deepest lying more than 33 feet (10 meters) below the surface. It also belongs to Malta's Bronze Age, but to a later period than Ggantija.

Glossary

archaeologist: a scientist who learns about the past by studying the remains of ancient objects and buildings

astronomical observatory: a structure from which people can observe and study stars, planets, and other objects in the sky

concentric circles: different-sized circles that have the same center

dolmen: a prehistoric monument consisting of two upright stones that support a horizontal stone across the top

domesticate: to tame; for example, to tame a wild animal so that it becomes a farm or household animal

epoch: a period in history

figurine: a small figure or statue

forage: to wander or graze in search of food

hereditary: passing directly from one generation of a family to another

grotto: a cave or a recessed place that resembles a cave

heelstone: the stone at the end of two lines of stone monuments

herbivore: a plant-eating animal

metallurgy: the science of blending and forging different metals

meticulously: very carefully

millennium: a thousand years

Neolithic: a period of the late Stone Age during which people used polished stone tools

parallel: lines that are equally distant from each other at every point

prehistory: times before there existed a written record of a people's history

sedentary: settled down in one place

summer solstice: the longest day of the year and the first day of summer, usually around June 22

Index

Page numbers in boldface type indicate illustrations.

Africa, 8
agriculture, beginnings of, 6-8, 12
Antequera, Caves of, 10
Asia, 8
Avebury, 26
Bretagne, France, **6,** 10, 16, **19,** 22
Britain, 4, **5,** 8, **8-9,** 10, **11,** 16, 18, 22-26, **31**
Bronze Age, 8, 14, 16, 18, 22, 24, 26, 28
Carnac, **6,** 18, **19**
Celts, 22, 24
Crete, 14, 16, 28
dolmens, 10, 22
Druids, 24
Egypt, 4, 16, 28
England. *See* Britain
Europe, **4,** 8, 10, 12, 16, 22
France, **6,** 10, 16, 18, **19,** 22
Galicia, 16, 22
Ggantija temples, **3, 5, 9, 15,** 26-28, **26, 27, 31**
Gozo Island, Malta, 26-28
Hal Saflieni, Hypogeum of, **15, 18,** 28-30, **28-29, 30, 31**
Iran, 14
Iraq, 8, 14
Iron Age, 22
King Arthur, 24, **24-25**

legends, 4, 24, 26, 28
Malta, **3,** 4, **5, 9,** 10, **15,** 26-30, **26, 27, 28-29, 30, 31**
maps, **19, 22, 26**
Mesopotamia, 8, 16
metals, use of, 12, 14-16, 18, 22
Middle East, 6, 10, 16
Minoan culture, 16
Minorca, **17, 20-21**
Neolithic Age, 4, 6, 10, 12, **12-13,** 16, 18, 22
nomads, 6, 8
Paleolithic Age, 12
Prescelly Mountains, Wales, 22, 24
religious practices, 6, 8, 10, 14, 18, 26, 30
Spain, 10, 12
Stonehenge, **5, 7, 8-9, 11,** 18, 22-26, **23, 25, 31**
Sumeria, 4, 16
tombs, 10, **19,** 18, 28-30, **28-29**
tools, 8, 14, 16, 28
trade and traders, 8
Turkey, 14
Valletta, Malta, 28
Valltorta, Castile (Spain), 12, **12-13**
Wessex Cult, 22
West Kennett Tomb, 10

Titles in the World Heritage Series

The Land of the Pharaohs
The Chinese Empire
Ancient Greece
Prehistoric Rock Art
The Roman Empire
Mayan Civilization
Tropical Rain Forests of Central America
Inca Civilization
Prehistoric Stone Monuments
Romanesque Art and Architecture
Great Animal Refuges
Coral Reefs

Photo Credits

Front Cover: Candy Lopesino & Juan Hidalgo/Incafo; p. 3: Lucio Ruiz Pastor/Incafo; p. 5: C. Lopesino & J. Hidalgo/Incafo; L. R. Pastor/Incafo; p. 6: Juan Carlos Lopesino & J. Hidalgo/Incafo; p. 11: C. Lopesino & J. Hidalgo/Incafo; Jose Manuel Reyero & Antonio Sacristn/Incafo; p. 15: L. R. Pastor/Incafo; p. 17: Juan Antonio Fernandez Durn & Covadonga de Noriega/Incafo; p. 18: L. R. Pastor/Incafo; p. 19: J. M. Reyero & A. Sacristn/Incafo; pp. 26-30: L. R. Pastor/Incafo; p. 31: L. R. Pastor/Incafo; C. Lopesino & J. Hidalgo/Incafo; back cover: C. Lopesino & J. Hidalgo/Incafo; L. R. Pastor/Incafo.

Project Editor, Childrens Press: Ann Heinrichs
Original Text: Ana Martin
Subject Consultant: Dr. Thomas F. Kehoe
Translator: Deborah Kent
Design: Alberto Caffaratto
Cartography: Modesto Arregui
Phototypesetting: Publishers Typesetters, Inc.

UNESCO's World Heritage

The United Nations Educational, Scientific, and Cultural Organization (UNESCO) was founded in 1946. Its purpose is to contribute to world peace by promoting cooperation among nations through education, science, and culture. UNESCO believes that such cooperation leads to universal respect for justice, for the rule of law, and for the basic human rights of all people.

UNESCO's many activities include, for example, combatting illiteracy, developing water resources, educating people on the environment, and promoting human rights.

In 1972, UNESCO established its World Heritage Convention. With members from over 100 nations, this international body works to protect cultural and natural wonders throughout the world. These include significant monuments, archaeological sites, geological formations, and natural landscapes. Such treasures, the Convention believes, are part of a World Heritage that belongs to all people. Thus, their preservation is important to us all.

Specialists on the World Heritage Committee have targeted over 300 sites for preservation. Through technical and financial aid, the international community restores, protects, and preserves these sites for future generations.

Volumes in the *World Heritage* series feature spectacular color photographs of various World Heritage sites and explain their historical, cultural, and scientific importance.